Nani and Jay Learn Finance

MONEY

Management

Budgeting
Wants vs Needs

**Written By
Evelyn Fernandez**

DEDICATION

I dedicate this book to the two people who has had the most influence in me becoming the woman I am today. To my mom and my husband, I love you.

The children are now 10 and 14 years old,
they are excited today because their parents will be
making a mall trip. Mom and Dad told them they
will be getting new clothes. Nani was imagining all
the new outfits she will get and Jay was thinking about a
new video game that just came out.

Another thing that popped in Nani's head was
an upgraded cell phone. Jay was also thinking about
other things he will buy. Even though they have their
own money, they figured their parents will get them
what they want as usual.

"Here we are, you guys ready to pick out some clothes?" asked Mom. "Yes," both children replied in excitement. "Great," said Mom. "Hey Dad, do you want to help me find the video game that just came out?" Jay asked his dad. Before Dad could reply Nani says, "great, so Mom and I can go look at the newest cell phone."

Dad is confused, "wait a minute what's going on here, didn't we come to buy clothes?" "You're right Dad, I wasn't aware that we came for other things," Mom adds. "We came to buy things that you need, not want," says Dad.

"But I really need the new game
because all my friends have it," said Jay.
"Right, and I really need a new cell phone
because I love taking selfies,
and the camera on mine is not the best," Nani says.

"Jay you do not need a new video game, because you have several that you haven't even finished yet, plus a video game is not essential. Nani, you do not need a new cell phone because your current one works just fine. A camera is an added perk to a cell phone," says Dad.

"We came to the mall today to buy you some clothes, which are essential, only because you've outgrown your current ones," says Mom. "What are essentials Mom?" Jay asks. "Essentials are things that we must have in order to survive, such as clothes, food, a home, and a car."

"A video game and a new cell phone are not items that are necessary to survive. Mom and I have to budget our money every month. This month we only have enough to buy essentials. Maybe next month we can budget other things," Dad explains.

"Ok now, what is a budget, this is too much,"
Jay says looking confused.
"A budget is when you add all your money together
and write down where all of it is going,
such as the lights, groceries, savings account,
the electricity, the house and things like that," says Mom.

"There is a difference between things we want and things we need. So, we should buy the things we need first, and see if we're able to buy the things we want with what is left. When you make good money decisions you will always have extra money for emergencies, and things that you like," Dad continues to explain.

WANTS

NEEDS

"Nani, let's say you have $60 dollars.
There are three things you want to buy.
A dress for your choir concert that is coming up,
a new phone, and more frames for your business.
This is when you need to budget your money
in order to make the best decision possible," says Dad.

Budget $60 Total

In order of importance:

Dress	$35
Frames	$10
Phone	$50

Dad breaks it down for Nani.
"The phone costs $50, the dress costs $35
and you need $10 for frames.
Now, we know that you need the dress for next week.
You do not need the cell phone,
because you already have one.
And you are out of frames for your business,
so you need more frames in order to make money.
What wil you do?"

"Uh, I don't know," Nani replies.
"Well, if I were you, I would write down
how much each item costs,
and put them in the order of importance,
then from there make a decision.
Actually, let's do that
together right now," Dad continues.
Dad pulls out a small notebook and a pen.

"Ok, I get it," says Jay, "let me answer."
"Nani, you must buy the dress,
because you have to match your clothes
with the rest of your choir next week."
Nani thinks she figured it out.
"I can buy the cell phone this week,
then buy the frames next week,
and buy the dress with
the money I make from selling the frames."
"What if you don't sell the frames
early enough to buy the dress?" Mom asks Nani.

Mom chuckles, "I don't think that would be the best choice. Let's see, I think you should go by the budget we just discussed. How many frames do you sell in one week Nani?" "I can sell about seven," Nani replies. "Ok, so seven frames sold at $5 each can make you $35 per week. I would buy the dress first, then buy seven frames, because that can earn you $35 next week. With that money you can buy the phone, but then you won't have any money left over to buy more frames."

Budget $60 Total

Buy dress first = $35 $60 - $35 = $25
Buy frames second = $10 $25 - $10 = $15
Sell 7 frames next week = $35 $5 x 7 = $35
Buy phone with $15 plus sales $15 + $35 = $50

"Mom is right, Nani. This is called budgeting. When you buy what you need before buying what you want. It is very important that is done in that order, so that you know exactly how all your money is being spent. When you become an adult, it will be a lot more confusing if you don't do this now," says Dad.

"When you know how your money is being spent you can make better decisions. Remember, when you want something you should ask yourself how will this benefit me? If you can answer with a positive, productive and beneficial response, then you can buy it, but if you can't then add it to your next month's budget. When you need something it's usually because it is essential. Don't forget to always add your savings as a need," said Dad.

"To avoid any surprises in costs and to be able to
buy yourself things that are wants
simply make a budget every month.
In the budget, calculate all the money you make,
what your goals are and how much it will take
to get to your goals." Mom adds.

"Dad and I make a budget every month.
Our budget always includes
how much money we made,
a list of everything we have to pay for
and what wants we have.
Here is our budget, maybe after seeing it
you can understand budgeting better," says Mom.

Nani and Jay only got the clothes they needed
that day. When they got home,
Mom and Dad showed them their budget.
The kids also each made a budget and were
excited to see how much they can buy if they just plan it.
They did not buy the cell phone or the video game,
but they did get it for Christmas.